Leading: from the Inside Out

DR. PRESTON B. RICH

ISBN: 154723010X
ISBN-13: 978-1547230105

DEDICATION

Just as birthing a baby requires a dedication to
God, I dedicate my first published book to God
who gave me the wherewithal to be able to think,
write, inspire, and lead. I would also like to
dedicate this book to my son,
Preston TB Rich II

CONTENTS

ACKNOWLEDGMENTS

I would like to thank all those who stuck with me through this entire process. Thank you for your patience, guidance, and love. .

1 INTRODUCTION

The 2017 workforce is experiencing the largest amount of transformational change as it has in at least 50 years. Four different generations are represented in the workplace and companies are desperately seeking a solution or "magic-bullet" to solve some of the prevailing issues companies are experiencing today. In addition, the increasing amount of lifestyle, racial, religious, and gender diversity in the workforce has left most leaders struggling to effectively lead teams, attract and maintain a committed workforce, gain and keep customers, sustain profitable businesses, and maintain their competitive advantage.

With all that is going on in the world in 2017, we are now faced with the reality that the unorthodox has seemingly become the norm. How do leaders navigate through the minutia and still take care of the most important corporate resource...the human being? How do leaders gain the most competitive advantage for the human capital that is invested in the company?

Human capital refers to the economic value of the combined knowledge, skills, and capabilities of employees. Since economists have now put a monetary value on the employee and investments into said employees such as education, training, and health, the focus has somewhat shifted to more of taking care of the employee than using the employee to gain more profit. With this supposed shift in focus to the employee, why are we still seeing an increase in unhappy workers, high absenteeism and turnover, and failing businesses?

I believe that the answer lies in the concept of understanding how leader behavior impacts organizational performance. More importantly, the ability of the leaders to relate to their employees and understand themselves. Leadership is defined as the process by which people are influenced to achieve goals. Organizational performance is defined as the measures by which a company determines if and how well the organization meets its goals.

The behaviors of the CEO and the leadership

corps are quantifiably linked to a specific impact on the performance of the organization. The CEO's transformational leadership behavior alone accounts for 56% of the performance of the organization. The leadership team excluding the CEO account for 41% of the organization's performance. When combined in statistical regression models, the behavior of the entire leadership team combined accounts for 62% of the impact on the organization's performance.

What does the scientific data tell us about the impact of transformational leadership and leader behavior on the performance of the organization? It tells us that since leadership is used to influence employees and employees are usually influenced by what they see, it is imperative for leaders to ensure that their behavior is transformational in nature and is specifically exhibited to encourage employees to accomplish their goals as well as the goals of the organization.

The method behind this transformational influence lies in the ability of the leaders to establish and maintain relationships, motivate their employees through said relationships by displaying critical thinking intellectual traits enhanced by character development, and employ effective communication practices to maintain a stable common-union with their employees.

Whew!!! That seems like a tall order, but if you break these concepts into smaller, more digestible components, you will master the necessities of leadership practice and be well on your way to becoming a transformational leader.

True leaders help followers realize their true potential and then remove all obstacles on their path to greatness. Sometimes you are the obstacle and gaining self-awareness is the key to the removal of that obstacle that is hampering your success as a leader. In my basic training squadron in the United States Air Force, our slogan was "Lead, Follow, or Get out of the Way", and I have learned over my many years of leading people, that this is essentially the key to experiencing success as a leader.

Have you ever wondered why most business students graduate colleges and universities with Bachelors and Masters of Business Administration degrees are not able to truly provide value to the organization until they have been employed for at least three years? Clearly after thousands of dollars and 25 papers later, the student is prepared to go to work and lead people, right? Wrong.

Some business schools have no clue about what is going on in the field. How can they? Their tenured professors have been walking through the halls of the colleges and sitting in their offices writing papers as a condition to keep their jobs set forth by the deans who have done the same. Much of the university business professorate have never worked in the field that they prepare students to enter, yet schools feel that because they have a "significant body of research", that they are better prepared to teach our students who aspire to become corporate leaders than veterans from the field with the same terminal degrees. That seems a bit sdrawkcab and is a flawed educational mentality. That flawed process needs to change ASAP.

Business schools should hire business professors who have been in the field of business. Do medical schools hire surgeons with no experience to teach other surgeons? Think about it. Why do you think that after years at the job, most companies pay to send some of their employees back to school to attend Executive MBA programs taught by leaders in their respective fields? Why do you think that schools are scrambling to find cybersecurity pros to teach in their newly developed cybersecurity programs?

Schools that offer executive business education have learned that whilst an earned doctorate and research publications may speak to a professor's intelligence, it may not be the only requirement needed to educate the new student demographic seeking to gain knowledge to obtain immediate gainful employment. Four-year business schools are losing their prospective students to two year colleges and companies that offer industry certifications as the red tape of academia hinders the schools' ability to change at the speed of the industry and their ability to meet the need of their customers…the students. Loss of students equals a loss of revenue equals loss of administrators equals a loss of professors equal a closed school.

School presidents and business deans should have the courage to hire scholars from the field who have the hands-on corporate experience to provide the students with real world scenarios about what they read about in their texts. They should do away with the archaic faculty committees that take an entire summer to hire professors for the fall semester. Faculty committees are fearful of change and seek to attract and hire professors who mimic their own characteristics which perpetuates a continuous cycle of mediocrity. These same professors then hold meetings with the school presidents to determine why student enrollment has steadily waned. Some schools have just posted solicitations for professors to fill positions two years in advance. Just as sure as you are reading this text, the field of academia will change where the students will demand to be better educated so that they can go to work when they graduate. Change is coming.

Yes; as a scholar, I have a passion for gathering research and writing papers but that is not what provided me with my experience as a leader. I received part of my leadership training from my parents. Ted and Norma Rich hold Ph.Ds. in the field of life and my only regret is that I did not learn how smart my father was until I was grown and out of the house. I gained even more experience from the United States Air Force when I enlisted at 17 years old about a month after I graduated high school and turned down three scholarships. My father had to sign my enlistment contract to allow me to enlist.

The rest of my management experience; mistakes and all, was gained at companies like Paranet, Sprint, International Network Service (INS), Lucent Technologies, Nokia, General Datatech, and PepsiCo. My experience trumped my pedigree. I got my first civilian people management job sans any formal degree. I was promoted by a man named Karl Houston who I like to say can make the Pope shake hands with the Devil as his collaborative leadership skills are unmatched. Karl needs to pursue a career in politics and he would solve the problems in the United States in 2 years. He hired me because he knew that I could lead people and he allowed me to miss some company functions to attend school at night.

The leadership education I received from "a day in the life" in corporate America was priceless. It taught me that not only do you need business acumen and relationship building skills, you need to know yourself as a person. From my experience in the field, I have identified a top problem that affects out businesses today. Business schools do not teach enough classes about the importance of knowing people, knowing yourself, and how to go to work the day after graduation.

This book is my attempt to address this problem by bringing awareness to the core principles of my mantra "People Before Business". In fact, those in my circle and students in my classes over the years have all heard me use the term. For companies to be effective in the new world economy with the most diverse business demographic we have ever experienced, the existing leadership profile must change.

Leaders can no longer be the autocratic, monolithic, transactional managers who worry more about strategy and profits than people. They must add to their skillset a transformational component that allows for the collaborative spirit of their workplace, suppliers, labor marker, and competitors to influence decisions. Gone are the days of "this is the way we have always done it" and "because I said so". The workplace is full of people who do not look, talk, worship, and most importantly, do not share the same thinking processes.

Effective leaders in 2017 are collaborative, critical thinking, communicative, self-aware, and transformational. They understand the importance of people and treat their employees like they are the most important resource in the organization. Now, some people are probably thinking, "well, everyone is not going to like the leader" or "yea, people are great, but profits keep the business running" and they are correct. At the same time, you must learn that disagreement is not bad if you are not disagreeable and profits are great if you earned them ethically by taking care of the people who generated profits for the company.

Is it better to be liked or effective? A manager once told me "Sometimes it is better to be nice, than right". I was perplexed by the statement, but after deeper reflection, he was not telling me to lie, he was telling me that the truth is self-evident which would not be any truer if delivered in a tone that offends. Yes, the 2017 world is full of people with sensitivities and almost nothing is politically correct, which further identifies the need for stronger leaders. In fact, I read a recent Harvard Business Review study that showed that people preferred a leader who got the job done instead of being likeable. I will watch this space as clearly this will change.

This book will introduce you to an approach to leadership that entails gaining knowledge of self, understanding how to think, consistently develop your character by communicating with the intent to gain and maintain a common union with your followers, understanding the social tier of motivation, and how to be truly transformational. To be a more effective leader and have your followers commit instead of complying, they need to have a firm belief that you are invested in helping them achieve their goals by making them better.

Please don't think that my stance on leadership is to give the people what they want without regard to running the organization as this is not my message. I feel that America has raised a generation of people who have a sense of unearned entitlement who want you to conform to the way they think blindly accepting their mentality whilst putting down your moral fortitude to make them feel ok. No. This is not my message. My message is clear. To be a leader in this world going forward, learn to lead from the inside out.

2 GETTING OUT OF YOUR OWN WAY

When leaders ask me for advice on how to be effective, I ask them if they have knowledge of self.   They look at me with peculiar facial expressions and then answer with "I think I do!". Knowledge of self surpasses all understanding. When I open my coaching sessions for a new class of client learners, I give a series of assignments that require each person to take the Kendall Life Languages Profile (KLLP) ™ and to write; or in the digital age, type a two-page reflection describing who they are. The first part is usually completed quickly because it involves a simple click to access the profile. The second part of that assignment is apparently not that easy to complete. People often ask me to help them get past their sticking points by first asking me why they cannot progress. I follow with these 5 questions:

1.   Who are you?

2.   Who do you want to be?

3.   What is stopping you from getting there?

4.   What are you doing to remove what is stopping you?

5.   Are you in your own way?

By the time we get to #5, they are ready to walk out the door and have called me about 20 things but a Child of God under their breath. "Who does this guy think he is asking me if I am in my own way?" they say, "Why did you ask me that Dr. Rich?", "Do I act like I am in my own way? My answer to the last question is always a resounding "YES!".

When I work as a coach to guide people past their sticking points, I make them face themselves. I believe that every person is created imperfectly perfect, uniquely amazing, and has something to offer that no one else in the world can deliver. The problem is that the learner does not think that way.

When people find themselves in their own way, it can be quite difficult for them to change. I advise my learners of the following 10 things. Feel free to read and heed if you feel that you are not living to your fullest potential.

1.   Release Negativity

People sometimes carry around negativity that; if not released, will kill their spirits, decay their minds, and cause them to eventually shut down. When you find yourself finding more fault in everything than being thankful for what you have and what you don't, you are carrying around negativity. Take a moment, or several during your day if you have a stressful job or home life to take a deep breath, take a nap, or just walk around outside and witness nature at its finest.

Witnessing nature makes us understand how insignificant we really are in the grand scheme of things. Have you ever thought that if all the world's insects died suddenly, that the world as we know it would soon begin to die as well? Likewise, if all the world's humans were to perish, nature would still survive and I dare say; thrive without our meddling...ashes to ashes...dust to dust. Negativity drains your natural ability to deal with stress and most importantly your ability to think. To get out of your own way, learn to release negativity.

2.   Learn to Forgive

In the Christian religion, we are taught to forgive those who do us harm or wrong. In fact, in Matthew 18:22, Peter asked Jesus if he should forgive people seven times and Jesus instructed

Peter to forgive seventy times seven times. Whoa...wait a minute, you mean to say that Christians are supposed to forgive people that many times? The answer remains yes, but when you forgive, nothing in the Bible says to trust man, especially after they harm you repeatedly.

Forgiveness is more for you than the other person. When you walk around with a heavy heart and hold grudges, you block what is positively destined to come your way. This is especially true if you seem to keep hitting brick walls and never getting what and where you want. Are you holding on to something that someone did to you? I can guarantee that the person who wronged you is not walking around with any guilt, especially if they are not aware of their past transgressions.

To be successful you simply cannot hold on to grudges. Forgive people, wish them well, and get on with your life. Try it. Call or write the person or people who wronged you that you have yet to forgive. Start off like this, "When you did _____, it made me feel like _____, and I have let it affect my life in this manner_____, but I will no longer let it affect my life so I forgive you and wish you well. You will feel better immediately. Remember, you are too great a person to be held back by someone else's past mistakes.

3. Harris' Law of the Windshield and Rear-View Mirror

One of my many mentors is my next-door neighbor, Mr. Norman Harris. At the time of this writing, he celebrated his 82nd birthday. Being the kind, generous, and wise Deacon that he is, he oft times blesses me with wisdom and knowledge. One day I was in the middle of one of my rants about how angry I had grown thinking about past events where I did not fare well. Since we were outside, he pointed to his truck and said, "look at that truck and tell me what you see". Quite naturally, I said "a truck". He just shook his head and began to tell me about the law of the windshield and the rear-view mirror.

If you look at your motor vehicle, you will find that that windshield is significantly larger than the tiny rear-view mirror that hangs in the middle giving the driver a clear picture of the back of the vehicle. This configuration reminds us that we should be concentrating on the things that are in front of us and not so much on what we passed. You see, the past is the past for a reason. We can never get it back so it is senseless to try to move forward by concentrating on the past.

Have you ever tried to drive down a street only paying attention to what was in the rear-view mirror? If you did, I hope your auto insurance was paid up and you had a competent auto body repair shop nearby. If you try to move forward concentrating on your past, you will most certainly drive yourself to disastrous destinations and dead ends.

Pay attention to all that is in front of you and you will be able to navigate through life's obstacles in a more confident manner. Never let your past hinder your forward progress. You should always remember your past to make sure you don't repeat the same mistakes, but if you are to realize your full potential and get out of your own way, pay attention to what you have in front of you.

4.   To Thine Own Self Be True

Too many times, people give up on their dreams because they listened and believed the advice of friends, family, members of the clergy, teachers, and anyone else who told them what they could not do. To those people, I say, if you can believe it, you will achieve it. The perplexing part of this dilemma is that some people give more credit to what others say than to what they tell themselves. Now, I am not saying to be bullheaded and take no advice from credible advisors, I am saying that your belief in your knowledge, skills, and abilities is all you need to be successful.

Sometimes, well-meaning individuals can

encourage you to give up on your dreams because you have not yet achieved your goals as planned. Usually, it is the people with whom we have established strong relationships such as parents, siblings, and teachers. New ideas often have several naysayers. Can you imagine what Noah went through when he started building an ark in the middle of a desert that was void of rainfall for a long time?

Sometimes, our loved ones have the best intentions, they just don't have the vision that we were gifted with and therefore they advise us to give up on our dreams simply because they cannot see what we see. After all, what is for you is for you and your visions are yours exclusively. Remember, you are uniquely amazing and what is destined for you is yours and yours alone. Live your destiny, not the next person's. If you want to get out of your own way, stay true to yourself and let your conscience be your guide.

5.   Keep Your Mind Open to Receive Your Blessings

Your thoughts become your words become your actions become your habits become your character, becomes your destiny. Simply put, your thoughts become your destiny. Since your mind controls all thoughts; keep your mind open and clear. Close minded people are not critical thinkers and we have all encountered these people. They seem to come out of the woodwork boldly and in droves; especially during election years. Close minded people are not necessarily concentrated in any specific political party, religion, sect, or other widely recognized affiliation. They only have one thing in common that brings them together...closeminded, uncritical thinking.

When you are seeking to become a better person, have a firm grasp of what you do not know, be able to intellectually empathize, and be a fair-minded thinker. This means that your mind should remain open to entertain new ideas that are not native to your belief system. I did not say that you had to agree or like the views of others, but to be an open-minded thinker, you have an obligation to learn to see the opposing side to every issue and understand how others can take an opposing stance.

Another major trait of an open-minded thinker is intellectual humility. Intellectual humility addresses your ability to firmly understand what you do not know. This is very difficult for some as they feel that they have achieved a high level of intellect through their academic pedigree. Many arguments could be solved if people would just admit to what they did not know and seek to learn to fill the knowledge gap. To be truly successful and get out of your own way, keep an open mind. You just might learn what you need to get to the next level.

6. Learn Things

NCIS New Orleans is a popular television series on network television that gives the viewer insight into the lives of the United States Naval Criminal Investigative Service set in New Orleans, Louisiana. The lead agent, Dwayne "King" Pride instructs his team; when investigating a case, to "Learn Things". To get out of your own way, have a teachable spirit and learn things.

Having a teachable spirit means that you are willing to adhere to tip #5 and keep your mind open to accept your blessings. I consider all learning as a blessing and have experienced the best lessons when I actively sought to learn new things. Your mind is the most valuable item in your possession as once you lose it, your life is essentially over. When you stop learning things, your development as a person is stunted and you begin to wallow in self-doubt, self-pity, and destructive behavior. An idle mind is the lab for negative thinking. Negative or "stinking" thinking destroys people very quickly and if it spreads to others, they too are destroyed.

Learning things entails actively seeking to obtain new knowledge about things that were previously unknown. You cannot possibly learn things until you have a firm understanding of what you don't know which is termed intellectual humility. Drs. Richard Paul and Linda Elder define intellectual humility as "having a consciousness of the limits of one's knowledge, including a sensitivity to circumstances in which one's native egocentrism is likely to function self-deceptively".

Why do you think the way you do? What experiences or human influencers shaped your intellectual perceptions of the world in which you live? Do you understand what you don't know? Are you willing to be transparent and honest with yourself? Before you attempt to learn things, make a conscious effort to find out what you don't know. After you discover the gap between what you know and do not know, seek to fill the knowledge gap. You will be a better person for yourself and the people in your circles. To get out of your own way, you strive to continuously learn things.

7. Don't Spend Major Time with Minor People

Minor people have a way of draining your energy. Most minor people spend their day wallowing in self-pity, having pity parties, and are going nowhere fast, but down. To get out of your own way, do not spend major time with minor people. How do you determine the people who are minor in your life? Anyone who does not support your vision, improve you as a person, or looks to constantly take your time, talent, or knowledge without pouring back into you are minor people in your circle. If you find that you are the smartest person in your circle, find a new circle.

The funniest thing that I have found in my short life is that people will get up in the morning, go through their routine, and leave their homes on the way to jobs that pay them for their time. Most people would not show up for work if they were not getting paid. Do you? By entering this social contract with your employer, you promise to give them your time, talent, and knowledge in exchange for a monetary reward. You expect to be paid for all the time you spend making money for the company faithfully expecting your check to be deposited into your account on an agreed upon interval. Why do you not follow the same rule with your personal life?

If your employer pays you a salary of $50,000 per year. They have in effect, agreed to invest $70,000 in you (50k + 40% employment burden of taxes, benefit payments, etc.). The company has recognized your worth as $33.65 per hour if you work 40 hours a week for 52 weeks a year. In this scenario, the time that you spend at work is worth $33.65 per hour and you routinely go to work daily until either you quit or you lose your job. Why do you agree to let complete strangers pay you for your time, but you give it away freely to people who have no interest in compensating you for your time?

Being compensated for your time with people usually does not involve the actual exchange of money. It does; however, entail getting something back in return whether it is an ear to listen, time, or consideration. The social exchange theory suggests that people in relationships often evaluate if they are receiving equal return for their energy expended to maintain said relationships. If you are a person who has done this and have determined that some people in your circle are not investing in you like you invest in them, it is time to deem them minor and move them out of your circle.

Moving people out of your circle may seem harsh, but just as a tree requires annual trimming to grow, so does your circle of people. You will never grow with people in your circle who constantly look for the worst before the better or the empty instead of the full. I suggest to my clients that they take an inventory of their circle twice a year and remove those people who are not beneficial to their cause or wellbeing. Remember, anything that is not beneficial is artificial and anything worth having is not easily obtained. If you want to get out of your own way, don't spend major time with minor people.

8. Show Me Your People and I Will Tell You Who You Are

Have you ever wondered why some people prefer to not associate with you? It may not have anything to do with who you are directly, it may have something to do with who you spend your time with. The term "birds of a feather flock together" is true. Like minded individuals often find themselves in a group or team and they start to operate in a groupthink mentality.

Groupthink is the concept that suggests that people in a group often forgo their objections with the direction of the group in an effort to "go along to get along". Groupthink is illustrated in the Abilene paradox, where a group of people collectively decided on a course of action that was counter to the preferences of many (or all) of the individuals in the group. Many times, people are caught doing things that they would not normally do or spend time with people they would not normally because of their inability to voice their feelings of discomfort and disagreement. This usually results in you being a part of a group of people who don't act like you...or do they?

My next statement is not intended to make light of crack addiction as any addiction in detrimental to the individual and people with addictions need to seek immediate help and need a consistent support system to break the addiction. If you hang around 9 crack addicts, you will be the 10th. Humans have a need to belong. Maslow's Hierarchy of Needs Theory states that people are motivated based on needs. I will explain more in the chapter on the social tier of motivation as there are other scholars who have posited the same concept. When you keep time and company with people who act certain ways, your need to belong takes over and you begin to take on their ways.

Take a moment to think about your circle of close friends. Most of you will say "me and my friends act very different". If that is the case, why do you have such close friendship? You and your circle of friends share a like-minded theme that is displayed in your actions and how you carry yourselves. Most people who observe you observe your group as well. Whatever the group does makes an impression on people who observe the group. This is the reason why people use the term "birds of a feather flock together". IF you want to get out of your own way, be aware of the company you keep as you will begin to take on the traits of the group. If the group acts in a negative manner, so will you.

9. Set Goals

Successful people will tell you that the reason they accomplished so much in their lives is because they set goals. Many people think that that goals are the thoughts floating around in your head that suggest that you need to get certain things done. Unless the ideas floating around in your head are recorded in some manner, they are just ideas or dreams that oft times never come to pass.

When setting goals, ensure that your goals follow the S.M.A.R.T. method. When you record your goals, you should make each goal Specific, Measurable, Attainable, Results-driven, and Time based. The SMART method is a tried and true process that increases the probability of achieving all your goals you set to accomplish.

Specificity is a necessity for the process of critical thinking. In fact, the intellectual standards of precision, accuracy, and clarity all speak to the need to be specific before you begin the thinking process. When you set a goal, make the goal specific. For example, I will walk through the SMART method on a simple goal. Step 1, name a specific idea like "I want to lose weight: Now, this is just the beginning as you can see that the idea is somewhat specific, but is not measurable which makes us not know it is not yet a goal. Step 2 involves placing a measure on what was created in step 1. Now the idea is "I want to lose 15 pounds". We have now added a unit of measure to step 1 as we progress to step 3 and determine that losing 15 pounds may be attainable. Step 4 shows us that losing 15 pounds is attainable and the result would be that the person is 15 pounds lighter...but by when? This is the last step in the SMART method where we add a unit of time and finally recording a true goal. "I want to lose 15 pounds by February 2018".

By following the SMART method to set goals, your probability of accomplishing your goals increases by 93%. Goals are easily tracked when they are drafted and set correctly. The path-goal theory suggests that a goal will be attained when properly set and planned for attainment.

When I worked as a project and program manager, I would be responsible for maintaining the project plan. The plan consisted of the steps necessary to accomplish an agreed upon goal or end state. Each item in the plan was linked to another item and all had times and dates attached. The dependencies for each step was clearly marked. Some managers I worked for were obsessed with the format of my plan, and my response was always the same "This plan is for me to track, not for me to make pretty for you". I said that to say this, if your plan outlines the steps needed to accomplish your goal, use any format you wish. The key is that the goal is SMART and you have put in the work to plan effectively to accomplish said goal. If you want to get out of your own way, set goals and develop plans to achieve said goals.

10. Change Your Thinking, Change Your Life

Figure 1 Thought-Destiny Chain

Thinking is the elemental start of everything we do as the highest order mammals on the planet. Our brains sit atop our central nervous system and control everything we do daily which also includes our involuntary activities which include breathing, blood circulation, and digestion. The way our system is designed; everything starts with a simple thought, yet many humans never take the time to consider how they think whilst thinking.

As I outlined in tip #5 above, I firmly believe that your destiny is inherently linked to your thoughts. Many people never take the time to evaluate their thinking processes. When I taught critical thinking in college, I would open the first class of instruction with two simple questions that I asked my students to complete. 1. The problem with my thinking is _____. 2. This has proven a problem in my life because_____.

Most students acknowledged that they had a flawed thinking process, thus the reason for taking the class, but occasionally I had a student who told me and the class that they had no problems with their thinking. These students never finished the semester in my class. Eventually, as I stepped through the chapters of the text, they realized that they were going to have to face themselves and apparently it was too much to bear.

Changing the way you think is an exercise in evaluating HOW you think instead of WHAT you think. To change your life, change the way you think and learn to consistently evaluate your thinking processes whilst thinking. At a minimum; to change your thinking, be open and willing to gain a firm understanding of what you do not know. You should be able to see the other or opposing side of issues where your stance is solid, and be open to becoming a fair-minded thinker. Fairmindedness is a state of thinking where you can thoroughly evaluate issues from multiple standpoints, make informed decisions based on clear, accurate, and precise data, and allow for disagreement without being disagreeable. To get out of your own way, have the courage to change your thinking to change your life.

3   CRITICAL THINKING

Drs. Richard Paul and Linda Elder developed a critical thinking model that includes essential intellectual standards and traits needed for the effective and efficient use of one of our brain's major functions; thinking. Paul and Elder found that thinking can be broken down in to steps based on experience and practice. The levels of thinking in figure 2 progress in practice from unreflective to accomplished. Paul and Elder found that unreflective thinkers are unaware of significant problems with their thinking and accomplished thinkers are said to be skillful and insightful where thinking comes to them as second nature.

Figure 2 Levels of thinking Paul, R. W., & Elder, L. (2002). Critical thinking: Tools for taking charge of your professional and personal life. Upper Saddle River, New Jersey: Pearson Education, Inc.

Effective leaders understand that leadership begins with their ability to change and adapt to change whilst influencing people to achieve goals. Effective leadership begins with thinking; and more specifically, critical thinking. Critical thinking involves the constant improvement of the individual's thinking process and it is the concept of how to think as opposed to what to think.

Drs. Paul and Elder have written several books about critical thinking and you may find their works; as well as an in-depth knowledge base on critical thinking, on their website www.criticalthinking.org. In their model of critical thinking, Paul and Elder suggested that critical thinking occurs when intellectual standards are applied to elements of reasoning to develop intellectual traits. Leaders should consistently question and change their own thinking in their quest to at least become a practicing thinker.

Intellectual Standards and Traits

Standards exist in nearly everything we encounter in life and most people accept those standards with little to no thought or hesitation. Did you know that standards exist for the way you think as well? Have you ever responded or reacted to something only to find out that you were wrong? In retrospect, do you think that you would have responded differently if you had known more details; the correct details, before you responded? This is what changing the way you think will help you to accomplish.

When evaluating problems, issues, and situations that require a response (all situations do not warrant responses), you should understand the accurate, precise, and clear information. Sometimes by the time we hear it, the data has been watered down and twisted so much that it completely conveys the wrong message.

When I am teaching about communication in my management classes, I engage the students in a game of telephone where I take a student out of the classroom to give them a complex sentence such as "The black cat, saw the yellow bird in the blue cage wearing a white hat". Each student is then to repeat the process by taking a classmate outside the classroom and conveying the same sentence. The last student finally has to write the sentence on the whiteboard. To date, the sentence has never been written as originally recited.

As a leader, you will be called upon to act as a mediator, confidant, disseminator of information, spokesperson to name a few and it is critical that you are able to respond intelligently whenever you are called upon to do so. Learning to think using the intellectual standards of clarity, accuracy, precision, and fairness will help you to answer the call when your team and managers need your leadership.

Paul and Elder suggested that asking when thinking with intellectual standards you ask yourself questions to help you think more effectively. "Clarity - Could you elaborate further on that point? Could you express that point in another way? Could you give me an illustration? Accuracy - Is that really true? How could we check that? How could we find out if that is true? Precision - Could you give more details? Could you be more specific? Fairness - Do I have a vested interest in this issue? Am I sympathetically representing the viewpoints of others?" By learning to think critically before making decisions, the risk of making bad decisions is significantly reduced.

Drs. Paul and Elder also developed nine

intellectual traits, but for this book I wanted to point out the specific traits that I believe are the absolute minimum to help you become self-aware of your thinking and to become a better leader. At a minimum, intellectual humility, empathy, integrity, and fairmindedness are the four intellectual traits that you should develop first if you want to be an efficient and effective leader.

Intellectual humility admits to ignorance, frankly sensitive to what you know and what you do not know. It implies being aware of your biases, prejudices, self-deceptive tendencies and the limitations of your viewpoint and experience. The opposite of intellectual humility is intellectual arrogance and a lack of consciousness of the limits of one's knowledge. Do you have any idea what or how much you do not know?

Leaders are brave enough to inventory their knowledge or depth of knowledge on all things. In 2017, it is completely possible that the manager is the person who knows the least about the task that his or her team is assigned. A leader has the courage to not only say "I don't know, but I will find out and get back with you.", they are also willing to be honest with themselves and acknowledge their level of ignorance.

When relating to individuals, especially followers, the leader is aware of biases, prejudices, and perceptions driven by said biases and prejudices. When leaders feel that their thinking is not in some way flawed, a problem will eventually arise in the execution of leadership duties. Humans are all a collection of their anthropological selves. Everything we see, hear, touch, feel, and taste all have equal potential to shape the way we think. For example, think about how you learned to get dressed, read, cook, or clean. Did you learn the process from your parents? Peers? Siblings?

I remember when I was a newlywed in our new home. I was stationed at Moody AFB, in Valdosta, Georgia and married my wife on the trip from RAF Lakenheath which was my last overseas duty station before I left the Air Force. No one at Moody was aware that I was newly married and the process for an incoming single Staff Sergeant was very different from that of a married Staff Sergeant. To add to the fray, I married a military member who was stationed at Lackland AFB in San Antonio, Texas who had not yet received any permanent change of station (PCS) orders.

Imagine me, a newly married man who just moved out of a dormitory on an Air Force base in England, having to find a home for my new wife and I without the luxury of having her in Georgia to approve my choice. Yes, approve is the correct word. For those reading this who are married, you understand.

I had to quickly learn what I did not know and try to expeditiously fill the knowledge gap. I had to start work, then find a way to get my wife to Georgia. Finally, the Air Force approved a permissive PCS where we absorbed the cost of the move. When she made it to the one level duplex I chose for us to live, she lovingly made it a home. I still don't think that she really liked the place but she smiled and did not make me feel bad for my choice.

One Saturday, I was outside cutting the grass and she was inside cooking breakfast. Our agreement was that I took care of the outside and she took care of the inside of the house. All was fine until I decided to tell her how to wash dishes. As you can imagine, you probably guessed how that went. I saw that she was washing the dishes and did not wash the glasses first. I criticized her and told her how she should wash dishes because "my mother taught me to wash glasses first". Her response was classic. She said "Well your Mom is not here but you are free to ask her to come here to wash these dishes, you do them yourself, or you can shut up and be happy with the way I wash the dishes, as long as they are clean, who cares about the sequence.

Jaded, chastised, and put in my place, I slammed a glass in the sink, acted like a 2-year-old, stomped, ranted, and cut my hand. All my immature behavior was simply a reaction to me not understanding my biases. Did I think my Mother was the only person who knew how to wash dishes? Why was I unaware or downright unwilling to see my wife's side? I was displaying intellectual arrogance and paid for it dearly. The funniest part of this whole story is that when I told my Mom about the incident, she agreed with my wife and further put me in my place, like only a Mother can. When you are not aware of your biases, prejudices, and ignorance, your ability to think critically is severely hindered. Develop intellectual humility by seeking to find out what you do not know.

Election years tend to bring out the best and worst in people. The 2016 United States Presidential race was no different. In fact, the 2016 Presidential race changed the face of the world. One candidate was a billionaire businessman whose polarizing words and actions brought about a new sense of American pride and activism amongst a cadre of people who felt as though their rights and privileges were quickly eroding. The other candidate, an experienced politician running on a Democratic ticket to be the first female President in United States history, was following a two-term African American President who happened to also be a first.

I would listen to the opinions and comments made about the Presidential race by my students, colleagues, and people in passing and I heard two distinctly different messages. Most of the opinions were shaped by the media and depending on which comment I heard, I could surmise which network influenced which. Fox News paid all its attention to the Republican candidate and MSNBC focused on the Democratic candidate. CNN tried desperately play the middle ground but had to resign to the "hot story" which was usually a reaction to something said by the Republican candidate that made the world look away and gasp "OH MY!!!".

All networks slanted their coverage for their dedicated demographic; after all, cable television is expensive and the networks had to deliver the news the way the viewers dictated. It almost seemed unfair. As a critical thinker, I watched rallies for both candidates, many channels of media coverage to include foreign coverage, read several national and local newspapers and was still confused on election day.

I realized that my best utility was served by voting my issues with my local politicians whilst casting my hopeful vote for the Presidential candidate of choice. November 8, 2016 was the day that turned politics, political pundits, advisors, experts, and the world upside down. On Wednesday morning, I heard and saw on social media outlets, the anger, discourse, denial, despair, sadness, and arrogance of both sides. I too was sad. I was sad because I realized that most people had no idea how to think with intellectual empathy.

Intellectual empathy is awareness of the need to actively entertain views that differ from our own, especially those with which we strongly disagree. It entails accurately reconstructing others' viewpoints and to self-consciously reason from premises, assumptions, and ideas other than our own. Leaders who develop intellectual empathy can disagree without being disagreeable in their attempt to make sound decisions.

What I saw was a complete reversal of fortune and commentary only this time, it was very biased towards the Republican President-elect. How quickly most people forgot that this was same reaction that the first African American U.S. President received in 2008. They forgot the insults, the shame, the disgust, the name calling, and the like. Some of the people who accused others of being racists and bigots in 2016 were the same people who called out and frowned upon the other side for acting the same way in 2008. The people who were against the President-elect displayed no intellectual integrity.

Intellectual integrity consists in holding ourselves to the same intellectual standards you expect others to honor (no double standards). Are you able to act in a manner that does not espouse a double standard? Can you hold yourself accountable the same way you hold others accountable for the same actions? To be an effective leader, hold yourself accountable and be able to evaluate yourself in the same way that you have the audacity to evaluate others.

When you hold others to a different standard than you hold yourself, you are conveying a message to them that you are better or "Do as I say, not as I do". This practice breeds conflict. Conflict needs two essential elements; scarcity of resources, and perception of power. Once conflict arises and is left unresolved, it escalates from criticism, to defensiveness, to stonewalling, to contempt. Contempt is a very difficult position from which to recover.

As a leader, you hold a position of power and when you are placed in charge of resources; human or otherwise, be very careful not to tip the scales of conflict. By governing yourself with intellectual integrity, you reduce the probability that conflict will arise and increase the probability of arriving at a solution if it does. Not only do you have to display intellectual humility, empathy, and integrity, to be an effective leader, you must display intellectual autonomy.

Intellectual autonomy is thinking for oneself while adhering to standards of rationality. It means thinking through issues using one's own thinking rather than uncritically accepting the viewpoints, opinions and judgments of others. Using the 2016 Presidential election again, we can clearly see where most people are void of the ability to think on their own. Please don't confuse intellectual empathy with intellectual autonomy as the two are distinctly different. One allows you to see the other side and the other allows you to own your own thoughts without blindly accepting opinions of those who may share the same.

I have heard some colleagues, strangers, and acquaintances alike state that they were going to the election polls and voting a straight ticket. Straight ticket voting is about the laziest method of voting in America and should be outlawed. Many times, people feel that their affiliations with certain groups and factions deserve a certain loyalty to remain a member. This practice is in effect dumbing down out nation and may be the reason that so many people benefit from programs that perpetuate the handout mentality of "feed me" instead of "teach me to fish".

Candidates of some parties have been in office for over 10 years whilst physically visiting their constituents in their home environments less than three times. How does this happen? It happens when people blindly, openly, and without question accept the opinions of others whom they feel a certain loyalty to because they heard the right "trigger words".

During the 2016 Presidential election, I was listening to the local urban radio station while driving to work. A political ad for a Democratic candidate came on asking for a vote in exchange for the promise of "ending institutional racism". Less than 3 minutes later, another ad for another Democratic candidate said the exact same thing. After carefully thinking, I became angry and sad at the same time. I wondered for who the candidates crafted that message.

I began to wonder what went through the minds of those candidates when they attempted to relate by conveying the message that they would "end institutional racism". A person who lacked the ability to generate autonomous thought would find these words favorable and immediately cast a mental vote for either candidate whilst eagerly waiting for election day to cast a physical vote. I did not. I wondered, "What is an Anglo-American male or female going to do differently to end institutional racism that a Black President could not do in 8 years?".

Whist this illustration may be a bit culturally biased, the fact remains that it happened. If you open your eyes to see things as they truly are instead of how you are told they are, you will begin to make discoveries about some long-held "truths" that you have adhered to since childhood. Question everything and never be afraid to think. Most corrupt leaders rely on your ability to be reliant on the leader's thoughts with no intervention from your own sound self-directed thinking.

What are some of the things that are in place today that you questioned in the back of your mind? Why does the United States have 9 Supreme Court justices to hear cases that could not be resolved in the lower courts but juries in the lower courts consist of 12 people? What if juries consisted of 9 people? Hung juries would be a thing of the past. Why are teachers paid less than judges? Public monies pay both but I'll bet you can all remember your favorite elementary teacher by name, but not the judge that heard your traffic, small claims, or divorce case?

Between the two, the teacher is paid less but had the most impact on your life, especially in the case of keeping you out of courtrooms.

The questions that you ask yourself in your attempt to become a critical thinker are important and essential to your development as a leader. Leaders are inundated with information and raw data daily at an alarming rate about several different aspects of their jobs. At all times, be aware that people who want favor from you will often tell you what you want to hear in hopes that you will blindly go along with what they say. Yes, trusted advisors who have been vetted tried and true may be excellent sources of data which may be accurate, precise, and clear; and as a leader, engage your own thinking to make a final informed decision. By taking the time to use intellectual autonomy, you will be a more effective and trusted leader.

All thinking should begin with the end in mind, in the effort to arrive at fairest point. Leader or not, we should all strive to be fair-minded in our thinking to make sound, fact based choices. Fairmindedness is being conscious of the need to treat all viewpoints alike, without reference to one's own feelings or vested interests, or the feelings or vested interests of one's friends, company, community or nation; implies adherence to intellectual standards without reference to one's own advantage or the advantage of one's group.

How then do you become a fair-minded thinker? A fair-minded leader? Until you learn to think, you will never become an effective leader. You cannot separate your leader self from your innate self. You are who you are. Changing your thought process will help you become a better person, communicator, relationship builder, family member, follower, leader, and the like. In everything you do as a person, you should strive to become a fair-minded thinker.

To be a fair-minded thinker, try to gather information from as many sides of an issue as are available to you. Be aware of the media that provides your information. Try to sift through biases and question how things are worded. In the past during the days of Walter Cronkite on CBS, the news was delivered without the opinion of the anchor. What you saw was what really happened.

Today, the media tends to slant their stories to fit their demographic as I mentioned before. For example, what some news outlets call "the celebration antics of overzealous sports fans" others would call a riot and vice versa. If you rely on the media to provide your information, make sure you conduct your own research before just accepting the media's opinion.

Every day, people sign up for leadership workshops, seminars, and classes in hopes that they will complete their training, earn a certificate, and become an instant leader. This is simply not the case. It does not matter what name is attached to the session including mine. Instructors can teach you everything in a leadership text and it still will not make you a leader. Leadership comes from within and everything you do to become or improve as a leader begins with trying to develop and change your thinking processes.

Leaders learn daily. Leaders take the time to develop their minds in scholarship and practice. To become an effective leader, learn to relate to others and give of yourself freely without expecting anything in return for your efforts except dedication from your followers to be their best. Think with intellectual standard and display intellectual traits that force you to see the other side and think fairly.

Leadership is not a one size fits all commission. It is a commitment to learning how to influence others in a manner that suits each follower differently. To be effective, learn to bend and flex to the needs of each person you lead. Are you able to consistently question your thinking process whilst thinking? Are you able to make fair minded decisions even when the decision may be in the favor of someone with an opposing view?

Remember that all things begin with a thought and your thoughts determine your destiny. Think long and hard about how you need to condition your thinking before you decide to lead people. Leaders can make or break people's lives and it is not easy nor should it be taken lightly. Military leaders who are ineffective get people killed. You will make mistakes along your journey, but if you keep a fair and open mind, empathetic heart, and act in an earnest and sincere manner for the good of your followers in your efforts to help them be their best selves, you will experience greatness in your leadership ambitions.

4   EMOTIONS, ATTITUDES, AND ACTION

If you want to be an effective leader for any significant amount of time, work to get your emotions in check. Cognitions, emotions, attitudes, and actions all work together and depending on how you control the sequential pattern of said components, will either make or break your success as a leader. It is critically important to be aware of your emotions and the effect they have on your behavior. Since I talked in the last chapter about thinking or cognitions, this chapter will be dedicated to the role that emotions and attitudes play in shaping and controlling your behavior.

Daniel Goleman developed the seminal concept of emotional intelligence (EQ) where he outlined four basic tenets that could help people become aware of their level of emotional intelligence. He defined self-awareness, self-management, social awareness, and relationship management as the four domains of emotional intelligence and outlines the importance of each domain as it applies to self-improvement. My book is not meant to give you a lesson on emotional intelligence, as his book is available in many formats and outlets, but I will give an overview to apply to your quest to become a better leader.

I truly believe that in-depth knowledge of self is the key component to your success as a person. This book is about leading from within and speaks to the importance of making a meaningful acquaintance with who you truly are, who you aspire to be, and the gap between the two dimensions. Yes, I refer to the states of individuals as dimensions because of the immense power people hold to change lives. Think about the people who have changed the course of your life with one speech, visit, or sentence. What innate power had been passed down to them from the universe? Could you possibly have the same power? The answer is yes.

People tend to think that successful people have some divine ordination that deemed them more powerful and dynamic than the rest of us mere mortals. Whilst this is not impossible for

God to do, most successful people that I have encountered have zeroed in on their greatness by being self-aware and understanding who they are. Being self-aware helps you to control your emotions and to better predict which situations are best left alone. Leaders gain self-awareness by soliciting feedback and conducting self-assessments.

Many people who claim to be self-aware are simply regurgitating or otherwise submitting to the labels that have been assigned them by loved ones, church leaders, friends, managers, and the like. For example, some students aspire to be lawyers because their parents and older siblings are lawyers. They hate to study, do not like to read, and hate taking tests. Instead, they are very creative and have the natural ability to paint, draw, and sketch. After years of flunking through law courses, the student decides to take an art class and is now a professional artist. Wouldn't that have been much more cost effective if the student took the time to become self-aware?

It is not easy to break away from predestined career and life paths that parents set for their children no more than it is to start school or enter the workforce after spending 18 years as a housewife raising children. If you are willing to take the time to get to know yourself, you will save a lot of time and probably a lot of money. Self-awareness also yields benefits in understanding how you react to certain people and situations.

Emotions are states of mind regulated by reactive feelings from situations or encounters that manifest themselves in our behavioral responses. Self-awareness as it relates to emotional intelligence is simply being aware of what you are feeling. Emotions are seldom; if at all, emanated from conscious effort.

Emotions may be positive or negative and if we are not careful, can cause us to act in a negative fashion. Whenever negative emotions freely control actions, disaster is imminent. Think about it, have you ever done something in a kneejerk manner reacting to something that you saw or heard and afterwards wished you had taken a moment to think before acting? It has happened to us all and until you learn to regulate yourself, it will continue to happen to you. Another domain of emotional intelligence is self-management.

Self-management is defined as the ability to control negative emotions and not allow anger to distract one's thinking away from the socially acceptable behavior or tasks at hand. This is especially difficult for younger people who have not yet begun to understand the power of anger, fear, and anxiety. Some people's ability to control anger, fear, and anxiety are so inhibited that they must take medication to do it for them. This instance is exacerbated if the person has experienced a traumatic situation.

When people find it difficult to control their emotions, they have a high probability of sabotaging their personal and professional lives in a predictable fashion. People who can control their emotions usually have an optimistic outlook on life and take setbacks in stride. People who are highly capable of managing their emotions are well suited to lead. People who are skilled at managing themselves are normally socially aware as well.

The emotional intelligence domain of social awareness speaks to the ability to practice empathy and recognize what others are feeling without them letting you know. In the last chapter, I discussed intellectual empathy where you must make a conscious effort to see the other side. With emotional intelligence, it takes this step a bit further in that you can sense what the other person is feeling.

Emotionally intelligent leaders rely on their ability to be socially aware as it relates to their followers. Sometimes, it is this skill that saves the life of a troubled team member seeking to find answers but afraid to expose themselves to the leader for fear of termination or reprimand. Your people must never be afraid to share when they are emotionally troubled. The sooner you get them help, the better it is for you, them, and the organization. Leaders pay attention to cues, know how to react accordingly to take care of their followers, and are not afraid to face problems head on. They seek professional help when needed. Leaders who are self and socially aware know their exact limitations and the limitations of their team members.

The final domain of emotional intelligence is relationship management. This domain identifies with the ability to connect to others, build and maintain relationships, influence others, and respond to their emotions. This domain really aligns with the essence of leadership in that it involves influence and social connection. One of the jobs of a leader is to influence others. In the execution of influence, the leader routinely works to maintain a common union with followers. This entails being available to provide guidance, direction, mentoring, and discipline when needed.

Leadership is impossible without relationships. This is especially true in today's workforce where four different generations are represented. The 2017 workplace is comprised of a diverse demographic that requires leaders to be emotionally intelligent, critical thinking, relationship builders. Gone are the days of "I say, you do". It is a place of collaborative team environments made up of the highest contingent of female workers ever. Females are the highest contingent in the workplace yet are the least represented in leadership and management ranks. In addition, women are still paid 18-20% less than their male counterparts in the same job capacities.

Minority representation has continued to rise, but still pales in comparison to their majority counterparts. This time more than ever calls for leaders to be culturally aware and receptive to workplace diversity and inclusion. With diversity comes a new set of rules that specifically calls for leaders with a high EQ. The leaders of the next ten years will have to be self-aware, culturally aware, relationship builders who are committed to treating their people like they are more important than profits.

When companies treat employees like cogs in a wheel, they suffer and eventually lose customers, suppliers, labor, and their competitive advantage. The leaders; from the top executives to the supervisors set the tone in organizations through the culture and climate. These influences have a unique impact on the attitude of the employees.

Attitudes are positive or negative evaluations that prompt a person to act certain ways. Leaders often take the most interest in attitudes about work and job satisfaction to preempt any negative employee activity. The funniest part about this is that the leaders themselves set the tone that controls job satisfaction among the workforce population. Leaders should know that negative behavior begets negative behavior. If you are a leader who seeks positive feedback from your workforce, invest your time and resources into making sure that your employee base is satisfied. Treat them like people to obtain commitment.

A popular example used by professors to illustrate the difference between commitment and compliance involves the breakfast scenario of the chicken and the pig. At breakfast, the chicken and the pig both provide food to the table except the pig is committed, whereas the chicken only complies. The pig provides sausage, ham, and bacon and is pretty much fully committed to the cause. The chicken only provides an egg. You want your employees to be committed to their jobs and the success of the organization instead of working in compliance with the social contract to receive a paycheck.

Leaders know the importance of having a

committed employee and the dangers of employing people who just comply. People who only comply have not fully invested in trusting the leader and in turn, waver in their support of the leader and the company. If this pattern of behavior continues, the compliant employee becomes a liability. Another problem is the psychological discomfort of cognitive dissonance where the employee acts in a manner that is inconsistent with their beliefs.

An example of cognitive dissonance can be seen in a scenario where an employee may work late hours but has personally committed to finishing night school. Another example of cognitive dissonance if an employee has stated that they are not fond of their leader or work, but act in an opposite manner in the leader's presence. If the leader is unaware of their employees' true thoughts, they risk losing employees who are not happy with their jobs. Leaders should always be aware of their employees' level of job satisfaction and the factors that control the employees' position.

As you can see, leadership is not easy. You must be aware of the social cues when leading people and you must be aware of how your actions set the tone for employee behavior. Employees; through the lens of social learning, pattern their behaviors after their leaders. Your job as a leader is to be aware of your behaviors as they significantly affect your employee population; and in turn, the performance of your organization. I will talk more about the impact of transformational leadership and leader behavior in chapter 7 of this book. To be an effective leader, understand how important it is for you to take care of the people who take care of your business.

5 SOCIAL TIER OF MOTIVATION

Motivation is defined as the reason or reasons one has for acting or behaving in a particular way. Leadership is defined as the action of leading a group of people or an organization. Leaders are tasked to motivate a diverse population of followers and most fail miserably because they attempt to motivate every follower in the same manner. Leaders are aware that all people are different, even people of similar backgrounds, gender, ethnicity, culture, and religion when attempting to motivate.

Scholars have developed several theories about human motivation and some have developed content theories that are primarily concerned with motivation as it relates to needs. Needs based theorists such as Abraham Maslow,

Clayton Alderfer, Donald McClelland, and Frederick Herzberg all suggested that people are motivated based on their basic need to relate or be otherwise socially affiliated with others. Leaders can use this information to become better and help followers to succeed.

Abraham Maslow developed the Hierarchy of Needs Theory where he posited that people are motivated as their needs are met in a stepwise fashion from the lowest order physiological need to the highest order need of self-actualization. Maslow found that as people's needs are satisfied, they progress to the next tier in the hierarchy. He termed this the progression principle. Likewise, when the need is no longer satisfied on any level, the person regresses to the lower order need thusly named the regression principle. Maslow also termed that the first three tiers, physiological, safety, and belongingness as the lower order needs and the top two tiers, esteem and self-actualization as the higher order needs.

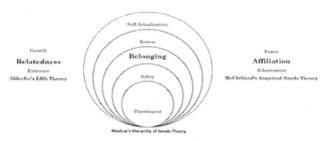

Figure 3 Illustration of the Social Tier of Motivation

In Maslow's model, the physiological level represents the most basic and foundational tier in that humans have basic physiological needs to survive. Humans need air, water, sex, and other physiological factors to sustain human life. The physiological tier is follow by the basic need for safety. The next tier that I call the social tier indicates the human's basic need for love or relationships. This tier is a part of my foundational assertion that humans are motivated by a basic need to relate with other humans.

When the need for belonginess is met, it not only satisfies the last of the lower order needs in Maslow's hierarchy, it sets the tone for the individual to aspire to obtain the need for esteem on the path to becoming their best selves or self-actualization. The final two needs of esteem and self-actualization are higher order needs in Maslow's hierarchy and are impossible to achieve if the need for belonging is not met. As a leader, if you want to influence your followers, help them satisfy their need to belong.

Satisfying your followers' need to belong does not mean that you are to have inappropriate relationships with them as this practice is unethical and leads to poor performance. Work to establish and maintain a stable working relationship with your followers. Figure 3 is a graphical representation of three needs based theories that emphasize the importance of the social tier of motivation. The ERG and Acquired Needs theories also point out people's need to relate.

Clayton Alderfer developed the ERG Theory that is similar to Maslow's hierarchy but different in that Alderfer's theory is not necessarily stepwise. Alderfer basically combined Maslow's bottom two needs into the individual's need for existence, and the top two needs into the individual's need for growth. The need for relatedness is again identified as an essential need for an individual's motivation and growth.

Effective leaders can tap into the individual's need to relate when they help others succeed. Your success as a leader is contingent on how well you motivate others to be their best. Many leaders are more concerned with their own success and ascension up the ranks that they forget to bring others along. Remember that if you are leading teams only to promote yourself, you will not hold a position that leads people for long. Great companies realize that the measure of a great leader rests in the achievements of their team members. Got it? Let's cover another theory to drive home the concept of using the social tier of motivation to lead people effectively.

The Acquired Needs Theory was developed by David McClelland who suggested that people gain certain needs as they progress through life and they learn of these needs from life experiences. The most frequently referenced needs are the need for achievement, affiliation, and power. Once again, we see that people have a need to form close personal relationships and have productive friendships.

Some people will say that they don't need people or that people are not important. Some people also say that they would rather be paid well than to have sound relationships. If you are a leader who hears your followers make these statements, know that they may be asking for your help to relate. People need to relate for motivation, personal growth, and true success. Some people downplay the need for relationships and overemphasize the need for money.

Countless studies have been conducted to underemphasize the role of money in the leaders' attempts to motivate employees, but some leaders still feel that money plays a significant role.

The role of money in motivation is miniscule at best in that whilst money may temporarily satisfy or motivate a worker, it alone will not keep the worker. Take for example the employee who accepts a job making $130,000 a year. When the worker accepts the position, he or she seems happy and content with their salary. For the next 6 months, the worker fulfills the social contract required and the leader feels as if the worker is committed to stay. One day, the same worker gets a call from a recruiter offering a job paying $160,000 doing the same thing and the worker accepts.

The leader now ponders what could be done to keep the employee and offers a counter of $170,000 but the worker still leaves the job. The leader; thinking the worker was committed, is now in a quandary because his worker is gone, intellectual capital has left the company and the long and arduous hiring process starts again. If you aspire to be a great leader, work to establish and maintain good working relationships that enhance your followers' personal growth that earns them recognition and responsibility.

Several texts that I have taught from suggest that job enrichment, rotation, and enlargement motivate workers to desirable levels of satisfaction. In my years of experience, I have never seen a successful implementation of job enrichment, rotation, or enlargement. From a theoretical standpoint, job enrichment, rotation, or enlargement is suggested to motivate employees, but it has never worked in any of the companies where I have worked as consultant or employee. Leaders need to understand that nothing can substitute a healthy working relationship between themselves and employees. People leave people, not companies or jobs. If you want to be effective as a leader, make a conscious effort to get to know your followers as people first, and resources later. Learn what motivates each of your followers and never try to manage people. Remember to lead people; and to manage sock drawers and checkbooks.

Learning your people can be as simple as asking about their passions, goals, and other aspirations. You could find out what matters to them. A simple method I used when I led teams was to ask myself the following questions:

Who matters?

What matters to who matters?

What can I do to facilitate getting what matters

to who matters?

You will find; as I did, that your people are just like you. They love what they love, like what they like, and have several different hobbies and interests. The key to taking advantage of the social tier of motivation is to treat people the way you would want to be treated without regard to the opinions of your peers, leaders, or coworkers. People are more important than your business because without them, the business would not survive.

Today's workforce has its own unique set of challenges in that this is the most diverse demographic the corporate America has ever experienced. Still, we have people who refuse to acknowledge the fact that many people in their workplace look, speak, love, worship, and play differently. In chapter 2 I outlined some of the intellectual traits needed to become a critical thinker and it bears repeating here. Keep an open mind and be willing to see the other side of all situations you encounter. Learning to be culturally aware, to embrace diversity, and to be inclusive helps you, your workers, and the company.

Most people grow up with a set of ideals or principles that were developed as they advanced through life. Left unchecked, many people grow up feeling as though their way is the best way an all others are foreign and wrong. Without proper exposure the different cultures, experiences, and people who are quite different, the person becomes a singly dimensional adult unaware of their own insecurities and counterproductive personality traits.

When people who are culturally unaware enter a diverse workplace, they begin to immediately compete for footing among the workforce searching to find people who look and act like them to form a protective bond. By virtue of the bond being protective, the unaware worker first begins to feel inferiority, but after their singly dimensional views are supported and hailed as correct, the worker begins to develop a complex of superiority looking to separate themselves from the diverse population. This is further fueled by the fact that they may work for a minority manager.

Eventually, the worker finds a way to be transferred, seeks employment elsewhere, or builds a coalition to have their manger demoted, removed, or terminated. Their work performance suffers, they become unapproachable, and begin to harbor feelings of entitlement and resentment driven by fear of the unknown. Instead of attempting to relate or allow the diverse manager to relate, the worker bides their time until their situation changes. In the off chance that they get promoted to a leadership position or find a leadership job at another company, the resentment for diverse workers continues and several capable workers leave the organization to get away from the culturally unaware leader.

This scenario sounds harsh and unbelievable, but it happens in top organizations at an alarming rate daily. If you wish to attract, and maintain top talent, ensure that you understand the importance that the social tier of motivation plays in organizations. Most importantly, accept your responsibility as a leader to care about your employees as much as you care about your paycheck.

6 LEADERS ARE RELATABLE

I have learned that everything we encounter in life is a direct result of a relationship. From the time we are born until after we die, everything we do requires some sort of relationship. Merriam-Webster defines relationship as the way in which two or more concepts, objects, or people are connected, or the state of being connected. Positive connection with other people is essential to motivating people as humans have a need to belong to or otherwise be related to other human beings. We cannot survive without some sort of relative interaction with another person.

Positive relatedness is scientifically linked to well-being and having a sound mind. In the chapter on the social tier of motivation, I explained how the content theories of motivation outlined how people were influenced by the satisfaction of higher and lower order needs. In this chapter, I will explain how the need to belong or otherwise establishing and maintaining positive relationships with other people affects the way a leader behaves and influences followers.

In 2008, I started teaching at Richland College in Dallas, Texas. In 2007, I graduated from Amberton University with an MBA in Strategic Leadership. I wanted to become a college professor. From the number of outstanding professors who taught me like Dr. Jack Cox, and the number of times I stood in front of people talking, I knew that I wanted to become a college professor. In fact, I was told that when I was a toddler, I pointed to Walter Cronkite on the television and said "Mom, I want to do that".

In my quest for a teaching job, I attended a job fair at Richland in 2008 and recognized my former business law teacher, Professor Randy Waterman who was sitting at the booth for the School of Business. When I stepped up to the table, she greeted me by saying "Preston Rich, I remember you!". I seemed to have made quite an impression on her in that I attended Richland as a student in 1998-1999. She took my resume and a week later, I received a call from the first person to ever give me a chance to teach, Dr. Linda Morable.

Dr. Linda Morable is the outstanding woman of

God and excellent professor who hired me to teach at Richland College in Dallas. She is the person responsible for introducing me to the college professorate and still serves as one of my most influential mentors today. She allowed me to fail without making me a failure as I learned to be a professor. More importantly, she introduced me to my academic uncle, Dr. David L. Ford Jr. who eventually honored me by sitting on my dissertation committee. One of the other things that Dr. Morable exposed me to was the Kendall Life Languages Profile (KLLP)™, the Kendall Life Languages Institute, and Mr. Fred Kendall.

Mr. Fred Kendall is the United States Marine who developed the KLLP which was; by his own words, a dedicated attempt by which he used to restore his family. He realized that his communication and actions; or lack thereof, was tearing his family apart and sabotaging his personal and professional life. He and his wife Anna created the Family Restoration Network (FRN) in Dallas, Texas and have been teaching the Life Languages for many years since its creation.

The KLLP has been found to be statistically significant and is a necessity for any person who wishes to understand themselves better. This communications profile shows people how they communicate, how character development affects their communication, and how certain stressors causes them to sabotage their personal and professional lives. If you want to take the KLLP, go to https://kllpme.com/DOCRICH, it will be the best $50 you spend in your life.

What does all that I just explained have to do with anything and how can what I just shared help you? Number one, character and communication determines your effectiveness as a leader because it plays a critical role in developing and maintaining solid relationships. I met Professor Waterman from taking a class, who introduced me to Dr. Morable, who introduced me to teaching in college, Dr. Ford, Mr. Kendall, and the KLLP. The latter is what I use to initially engage with my coaching clients today. In a way, my relationship with Professor Waterman was critical in my development as a professor and is still providing me with residual value today.

The second thing to be gained from my short story is that the results from the KLLP taught me how strong character shapes your destiny. I firmly believe that your thoughts become your words, become your actions, become your habits, become your character, becomes your destiny. As a leader, you should strive to continually develop your character as character development is a daily activity. Mr. Kendall told our certification class that to the degree that your talent, charisma, education and success exceed your character development, will be the degree that you fail. To the degree that your CHARACTER exceeds your talent, charisma, education and success, will be the degree that you have TRUE SUCCESS.

Merriam-Webster defines character as the mental and moral qualities distinctive to an individual; one of the attributes or features that make up and distinguish an individual; or the complex combination of mental and ethical traits marking and often individualizing a person, group, or nation. Most elements that involve self-improvement are linked to the way you think and act. Mental qualities distinctive to an individual speak to how a person thinks. Moral qualities speak to the way a person acts. How you think and how you act will determine your level of true success in life. How you think and act will ultimately determine your destiny.

If you were to think about some of the most successful people in the world, you would see that they had strong character that helped them endure the most difficult of times. Some people define success as being wealthy and having the ability to buy any material thing they desire. True success lies in the ability to accomplish your goals, help others, and leave this world better than it was when you were here. After all, I see no U-Hauls in the cemetery so I surmise that material things just stay here when we die.

Character development is a key component of a person's ability to be truly successful. I have seen several athletes, musicians, and other wealthy people who were at the top of their respective games only to lose their wealth or keep their wealth and lose their people because they had less than desirable character. Developing character is essential to personal development and should be a daily undertaking for anyone wishing to be a great leader.

How does one develop their character? How does one develop the complex mental and ethical traits needed to realize true success? To develop your character, it is critical that you have a firm understanding of the definitive concept of strong character. Having strong character means that you are the type of person who stands behind your belief system, takes responsibility for your actions, and treats all people with respect. This is not the end all to be all exhaustive list of things in the recipe for character development, but it is an excellent starting point. When a person has a fundamental understanding of who they are, they begin to peel away the layers that exist between who they are and who they want to be.

Learn how to treat others as you would want them to treat you in your effort to become person that others wish to emulate. Learn how to allow yourself to learn from your mistakes, take constructive criticism, and be an intent listener. Trust yourself before you ask anyone else to trust you. Have a firm understanding of what you do not know. Finally, have a relationship with yourself before you ask anyone else to do the same. These are the things that help you develop strong character and a high degree of emotional intelligence.

You should aspire to be a person of sound and strong character who uses his character traits for the good of others. Understanding what is good for others starts with the ability to empathize with another person to obtain a further understanding of their position in life. When you learn to show empathy and even display intellectual empathy, you will be well on your way to developing strong character.

Your character development is also critical to your survival as a leader. Leaders wear many hats and are oft times asked to compromise their values for the good of the organization. Leaders never allow a paycheck to put them in an ethical dilemma where their character is compromised.

Social awareness or empathy is essential to developing character as it helps one see the other side. Understanding the world around you can help you ensure that you at least start thinking about the other person's perspective. Why is this important? Well, unless you live alone in a box and interact with no other humans, you will constantly engage in social exchanges with people. Some of these people may not share your views, values, or beliefs. Learning to see their side; not necessarily agreeing with the other side, but at least seeing the other side is critical in your efforts to develop your character.

Communication is a process that consists of; at a minimum, the sender, channel, message, receiver, and feedback in our attempts to establish common unions with others. The way you communicate will determine your level of true success or failure as a leader. Leaders rely on their communication skills to relay information and to primarily influence followers to complete certain tasks. Learning how you communicate to who is another critical aspect that you need to know if you want to be an effective leader.

When you begin to communicate with another person, you should always seek to learn their communicative preference before undertaking the task. If you are not aware and are given no cues as to how the other person prefers to communicate, a simple gesture showing them that you care to know usually suffices. A simple hello may break the ice, but gives you no more insight about them than you had before you spoke. Engage in conversations that make it easy for the other person to share. Search for an understanding of your followers before you ask for their understanding of you. Franklin Covey says to "seek first to understand than to be understood".

When a leader can put down his or her need to be heard or understood, feared, or revered, it creates an atmosphere of sharing that is inviting and serene. Many communication barriers are torn down when leaders extend themselves or are otherwise willing to be vulnerable to help others.

I have consistently stressed the importance of the relationship. I have given you an example of how my relationships worked to my advantage, and now I will explain how building your network is contingent on your ability to be relatable. Think about the last three products or services purchased where you walked away happy and satisfied. Can you remember your sales representatives name? Now think of time you did not walk away happy or satisfied. I would venture to say that the former transaction was the better transaction because you built a relationship with your sales representative.

People do business with people that they like…plain and simple. I have been in companies that employed top experts galore but the customers only wanted to deal with one individual. You can have more degrees than a thermometer and more certifications than the board of health, if you are not likeable, you will not be successful. You must be a likable person so that others are willing to work with you.

As a leader of a professional services organization, I was tasked with a team of network analysts who were highly skilled technical gurus with equipment manufactured by Cisco Systems. Most customers had their favorites and preferred to work with only these analysts on their projects. Some clients made demands at the most inopportune moments which always produced a "teachable moment".

One day, I received a call from an irate client who ran into an equipment failure and needed his new equipment configured for replacement to bring his network back to full capacity. He specifically asked for analyst X, who happened to be on vacation out of town. He read me the riot act and told me that I had better get analyst X; and only analyst X, at his location ASAP or he would sever the contract and find another services vendor. I let him finish his rant and began to ask questions to find out more information about his issue.

I knew that I was not calling my analyst from vacation and I also knew that the client was not going to sever the contract as this would have put him in a more severe situation. I calmly told him that analyst X was on vacation, but analyst Z was available. Analyst Z was more experienced and helped analyst X configure the original equipment unbeknownst to the client.

To remedy the situation, I immediately called analyst Z to my office; which had no doors as a requirement of the CEO, and allowed the two a chance to converse about the issue. Analyst Z went to the client's locations and saved his day. I did not charge the client for that emergency issue because I valued the relationship more than the money we would have received for the emergency service. Instead, I waited a week and asked the sales manager to offer a maintenance services package to the client to cover any further situations which was a more economical choice. The client agreed to purchase the package before the sales manager hung up the phone.

The major play in this example was that all parties involved were relatable. The client was happy with the relationship with the analysts, me, and the sales manager. Truthfully, the account manager owned the relationship and I had to ensure that me and my analysts kept the relationship favorable. Account managers hate nothing more than a technical analyst jeopardizing a long-standing relationship.

Leaders should be aware of all relationships that they may influence in their professional and personal lives. I guess you are wondering what personal relationships have to do with professional relationships. The key is that you are you wherever you go and no matter how small your network, actions you take to sabotage your personal relationships; either intentional or not, will eventually spill over into your professional relationships. It is critical to govern yourself accordingly. It only takes one "aw shucks" to destroy a million "pats on the back". Once a relationship is compromised, it is very difficult to recover. Protect your network by any means legally, morally, and ethically necessary.

Lions don't need to roar no more than leaders need to outwardly proclaim their power in leadership roles. Leaders do so in their actions and attention to detail in developing others. Please understand that as a leader, your purpose is to make others better, not to use them to glorify yourself. Most leaders who glorify themselves are only leaders by name and not action. When I hear people say, "I'm a great leader", I cringe and feel the hairs on my neck stand up as they immediately confirm that they are no more a leader than I am an opera singer. To be a relatable, effective, and efficient leader, check your ego at the door.

In my opinion, all forms of leadership involve a teaching and learning relationship. The leader-follower connection is a one to many relationship in that one leader can affect many lives exponentially. It is imperative that you ensure that what you say and do is noteworthy, useful, and can positively develop your people. Andragogy is the method and practice of educating adults. One of the major keys to doing so effectively is to put down your ego. Adults who follow you do not need to constantly hear about your accomplishments, accolades, and pedigree. Say it once and start the practice of leading.

I once worked at a small private computer networking company as a project manager. I was hired to be a project manager and after the successful completion of my project, I was promoted to managing consultant. On the day I was promoted, we were acquired by a large telecommunications company. I was assigned a team of 23 people from the acquiring organization. The first question they all asked was "We bought your company, why are you my boss?". Perplexed and armed with only a title and backing from my managing principal, I immediately began to look for ways to relate to my new team.

I held a meeting with the team via conference call to make a short introduction and asked for help in getting to know who they were. I let the team know that I was dedicated to keeping them protected and let them know about my "Richisms" which were 1) Never get me blindsided, and 2) No one messes with my people. In the conference call, I scheduled a face to face meeting with each of them to complete their professional development plans.

The professional development plans were actual documents that outlined their 6 month, 12 month, and 2 year goals as well as the plans to accomplish said goals. This plan was a signed and agreed upon plan that documented their outline of all professional development classes that they were required to take. I developed six internal courses and branded them the "Rich Six". Each person was responsible for completing the classes and ensuring that the courses were completed in a year. We met again at the 6 month point to track progress and finally at the 12 month point for merit reviews which usually resulted in raises for each member who completed their assigned tasks in the agreed upon plan.

When I inherited this team, it consisted of 6 remote members who were serving customers in cities other than those in the Dallas-Fort Worth metroplex. I got permission from my manager to travel to each person to meet face to face. This experience proved to be most helpful in that it showed each person that I was genuinely interested in getting to know them and to ask them what I could do to make them better.

In this instance, as with most, as a leader, I had to put down my ego and make myself vulnerable to my team. This was a bit daunting at first thought, but as I met with each person on my team, I gained commitment. I only lost one person on the team who quit before I could travel to meet him in Chicago. My teams excelled and consistently delivered high revenue and value to the organization. In checking your ego at the door as a leader, be vulnerable, transparent, and have a teachable spirit.

Leaders are often tasked with the practice of disseminating information, but some concentrate more on the downward communication than accepting upward and lateral information. Communication can also be referred to as the establishment of a common union in that one strives to ensure to always maintain positive rapport. With the components of communication being the sender, channel, message, receiver, and feedback, some leaders either disregard or otherwise choose to ignore feedback directed to them. When leaders feel as though they are incapable of receiving constructive criticism and feedback, they are said to have an unteachable spirit.

The best leaders have a teachable spirit and constantly seek to develop themselves. They read at least 2 books a month, watch webinars, attend lunch and learn sessions, and learn something new from their team. They are willing to be the student and humbly dedicate themselves to interpreting a "day in the life" of their team members.

One of the first steps in checking ego at the door is admitting that you do not know all things. Leaders make themselves and the company look bad when they shift the focus on themselves instead of leading people. Inflated leader egos sink organizations. If you want to be a great leader, learn to let others shine. Routinely use words like, "we", "our", and "the team" and not "I", "mine", and "me". Lions don't need to roar as they are the undisputed kings of the jungle.

7 TRANSFORMATIONAL LEADERSHIP

Transformational leadership is a leadership process distinguished by the ability to create vision, bring about innovation and change, and build relationships that provide meaning to followers who actively seek to become their best selves. Transformational leaders are in high demand in that today's workforce has changed to that of a dynamic, social, fast paced nature.

The speed of change in today's businesses dictate the need for a type of leadership that does more than just tell people what to do, it requires a leader who is self-aware and interested in bringing people along. Transformational leaders increase the chances that organizations experience success in that they work to implement organizational change.

Transformational leadership is based on four tenets or 4 Is, idealized influence, inspirational motivation, individualized consideration, and intellectual stimulation. Each tenet represents a basic theme that dictates the actions that leaders should take to display transformational leadership behavior. Notice that each component serves a unique purpose which are collectively dedicated to the process of positive development of the follower.

Idealized Influence (II) speaks to the leader's capability to serve as a role model and the fact that followers admire and want to emulate the leader's behavior. In fact, the attributions made by followers and colleagues as well as the leader's behavior are both subcomponents of idealized influence that represent this tenet's interactional nature. Transformational leaders are collaborative and are constantly aware of their behavior and their role in the follower's social learning process.

Inspirational Motivation (IM) is characterized by the actions of the leader to influence followers to visualize a future state. The transformational leader provides a challenge and meaning to the follower's work. The leader articulates the vision and gains commitment from the followers in their quest for achievement and purpose. Inspirational motivation coupled with idealized influence are what constitute the transformational leader's charisma.

Transformational leaders demonstrate genuine concern for the needs and feelings of followers. This describes the tenet of Individualized Consideration (IC) and speaks to the leader's ability to give each follower personal attention in a coaching, mentoring, or teaching capacity. The leader accepts the individual differences of the follower and allows for the natural progression of the follower's level of growth. The leader treats each follower individuals with uniquely different needs.

Intellectual Stimulation (IS) entails engaging the follower's ability to think critically. The leader teaches the follower how to think instead of what to think. Transformational leaders encourage the follower to develop problem solving creativity by encouraging the follower to question assumptions to find new ways to solve old problems. The leader welcomes and allows the follower to make mistakes to help them understand the importance of thinking differently by utilizing intellectual standards whilst developing intellectual traits.

What does this all mean? Does the leader need to be an MBA to understand transformational leadership? The answer is NO. Transformational leaders know that giving of themselves is a critical necessity in their efforts to inspire their followers' quest for greatness and self-actualization. Some argue that the developers of the transformational leadership theory stopped short of the abundance of the beneficial aspects of finding and developing followers.

Why does transformational leadership matter? What difference does leader behavior make on the performance of the organization? Plenty. I conducted a study to identify the extent of any relationship that existed between ethical leader behavior, transformational leadership, and organizational performance. From the results of the study, I concluded that a statistically significant relationship existed between ethical leader behavior, transformational leadership, and perceived organizational performance.

Transformational leadership was found to have more of an effect in explaining variance in perceived organizational performance than did ethical leader behavior. This finding introduced a profound and interesting notion that employees may pay more attention to the actions of the CEO than the actions of their direct managers at every level in the organization. It also suggests that the actions of the CEO have more of an impact on organizational performance than the behavior of the employees' direct managers.

Want actual scientific numbers? OK, when explaining the amount of variance in perceived organizational performance, transformational leadership accounted for 56% alone. Ethical leader behavior accounted for 41% alone; and when regressed with transformational leadership, significantly changed the effect by only .059 to produce a combined effect of explaining 62% of the variance in perceived organizational performance.

The findings in my study have shed light and provided validity to the previous claims that the organization's success depends heavily on the behavior of the chief executive. Organizational theory has also led many scholars to believe that ethical leader behavior greatly influences organizational performance. The CEO sets the ethical tone for the organization; and in many organizations, the non-management employees are at least three levels away from said CEO.

The middle manager or direct manager is believed to have the greatest effect on the employees' behavior and that effect is usually attributed to ethical leader behavior. The results of this study suggest that ethical leader behavior is a significant predictor alone, but only accounts for a very small significant change in the explanation of the variance in perceived organizational performance when combined with transformational leadership.

The data from my study lends scientific proof that transformational leadership has the highest impact on employees. The behavior espoused in transformational leaders inspire followers to perform in a positive manner resulting in higher levels of organizational performance. Companies must invest to develop transformational leaders in the middle and line manager ranks to attract and maintain a committed workforce. If you want to be an effective leader, learn to be transformational in all aspects of your life.

In today's world environment, with the sudden increase in the constant questioning of ethical leader behavior, it would be prudent to study the potential reasoning behind my study's finding that the combination of ethical leadership and transformational leadership has no significant effect on organizational performance. A proposed study could be designed to understand how each of the components of the interaction contributes to the non-effect on organizational performance. Another recommendation for future research rests with the understanding of how age, gender, and company tenure affects the perception of organizational performance. This type of study may have to be more qualitative in nature to truly understand what the employee thinks or feels about company performance and how leader behavior influences their cognitions and emotions.

Ethical leader behavior is a complex construct that consists of many subcomponents that could be used to explain why leaders act in the manners displayed in organizations. More complex is the understanding how ethical leader behavior affects the bottom line of corporations and governmental agencies. My study contributed to the field of knowledge a measure that can be used to begin to evaluate the quantitative effect of leadership behavior on organizational outcomes. The results of the study provided scholars with a platform by which to base new theoretical assumptions in the arena of ethical behavior and transformational leadership, and using these variables to explicate their effect on objective corporate and public-sector results.

Ethical leader behavior greatly influences organizational performance although not as much as does transformational leadership, but little is known about how the influence is extended. Corporate culture has been theorized to have some role in the advancement of organizational behavior, but has failed to be measured in a way that can offer any explanation as to its relationship in the advancement of behavioral influence. What is the vehicle that drives employees to act in organizations? How does the employee interpret the actions of direct, middle, and senior managers? What causes the leader to behave in different ways? Why does transformational leadership contribute more to explaining perceived organizational performance than does ethical leader behavior?

The research leans heavily on innate leadership traits in determining a leader's ability to motivate and influence people, but the answer to questions about ethical leader behavior may rest in understanding the personal moral core of an individual when assuming a leadership role. The leader's effect on people may have more to do with organizational performance than once thought.

A leader's success in an organization may rest with his ability to relate with other people in the organization that share a common moral fiber or ethical bond. This ethical bond may be the main contributing factor in determining how the employee will act in the execution of job duties to help the company reach its business goals. The shift from business results to people results may prove to be a new method of making and keeping companies successful. A concentration on transforming and leading people may be the key to understanding how to reduce turnover rates, absenteeism, and unethical behavior while promoting steady growth and increasing corporate longevity in its industry.

8 LIFE

Adversity is defined as a state or instance of serious or continued difficulty or misfortune. If you spend enough time on this earth, you will experience your fair share of adversity and how you deal with each instance will prove to be definitive moments in your life. I believe that adversity has shaped my way of thinking as well as my approach to life, leadership, and relationships. I also believe that I am where I am in life because of prayer, God's Plan, my choices, and the people in my life.

I was born in Washington, D.C., and grew up in Norfolk, VA. I saw my parents work two and three jobs to support me and my younger sisters. Their work paid off as my siblings and I all grew up, held jobs, and graduated from college. My parents primarily raised us in the predominantly African American suburban community called Poplar Halls. I attended elementary and middle school at St. Mary's Academy and went on to attend and graduate from Booker T. Washington

High School in Norfolk. I enlisted in the Air Force at 17 years old and my life changed forever.

If you were to subscribe to some media outlets and listen to some Americans, one would think that the military is a place of harsh realities and warmongering generals who want to bomb anything that does not support the American flag. Whilst some of that is true, it is in the very small minority, but if anyone thinks that protecting freedom does not sometimes require that the United States military act harshly, you are sadly mistaken and misinformed. After all, we enlisted to defend the Constitution against all enemies, foreign and domestic. The United States military has always protected, and will continue to protect the freedoms of this great nation by any means necessary.

My service in the United States Air Force played an integral role in my development and maturity as a man, but my foundation was laid by my late father, Theodore Rich (he didn't play). I spent 10 and a half years in the Air Force and enjoyed every minute. I traveled the world several times and experienced more in those 10 years than most people will experience in a lifetime. I was deployed to support Operation Desert Storm and served in the primary area of responsibility (AOR). Most importantly, I met adversity head on, had my share of disappointments, experienced the power of prayer in action, experienced true love, and forged relationships that are still very much in tact today.

As an educated African American man, I have experienced my share of disappointments. Some of those disappointments came from outward displays of racism and most were due to my lack of preparation and my expectation that someone else would care more for me than I did for myself. Some people reading the first line of this paragraph may say, "Why did he have to mention that he was a Black man, why couldn't he just say that he experienced disappointments as a man?". I will tell you that I am speaking from my experiences as a man, and I am African American. I can only speak from my past experiences as I saw them through my lens.

I have seen some Anglo-American people take offense when minorities call attention to their racial differences citing that this practice breeds racism. To those that do, I ask you to trade places with a minority for one day. One day I asked the Anglo-American students in my class if they thought African Americans were treated fairly in America and most agreed. I then asked them if they would trade places with an African American today and the answer was a collective and emphatic, "no".

I wondered "Why not trade places if we all receive fair treatment?". Leaders appreciate perspectives that originate from diverse people and experiences. Most importantly, effective leaders appreciate diversity of thought and the lens in which others see the world. The old saying "until you walk a mile in my shoes..." still applies today. Leaders who desire to be successful must be able to respect and appreciate the opinions of others who have experiences completely different than their own.

No, I did not bring up that point to gripe and moan about unfair treatment of minorities in America as that song is old, tired, and serves no purpose in making positive progression towards solving the problem. The truth is that some people in America have a problem with minorities and I believe that they themselves are a minority. There, I said it...now what? Never spend your time complaining about anything. Put your big boy and big girl underwear on, decide to achieve your goals and like Nike's slogan says, "Just Do It"! I believe that my job as a leader is to help people achieve their goals despite their adversities.

The first step in beating adversity is to recognize the issue and be a part of the solution.

If you are not part of the solution, you are part of the problem. The days of "they don't like me because I am a different color" are over. I ask my mentees, "What does knowing that some people won't like you simply because of the color of your skin have to do with your levels of achievements in life?". Nothing, if you change your thinking. Trying three times as hard as the next person should become commonplace and never let what someone else thinks about you impede your progress. Adapt and overcome.

I was always told by my parents to try three times as hard as the next person, but some things were always easy, like getting good grades in high school. Getting a "C" was passing, but why not strive to get an "A"? In my sophomore year of high school, I decided to try to be "cool", skip class, not complete assignments, and be disrespectful to teachers. I had home training and knew that I was wrong, but I just wanted to be like my "friends". I ended the year with a 1.6 GPA and had to attend summer school to bring up my GPA and progress to the 11the grade. In the Norfolk Public School system; much like many school systems, summer school attendance was fee based.

I asked my parents for the money and I will never forget my mother's words, "I don't care if it takes you until you are 21 to finish high school, you decided to flunk, you pay for summer school yourself". I was shocked! How could my mother say such things? I was her oldest child, her only son. How could she say this to me? The funniest thing was when I went downstairs to ask my dad for the money, his response was "What did Norma say?". I was devastated. How dare my parents not get me out of a situation I put myself into? It shouldn't matter that I spent September to June blowing off FREE school...right?". WRONG!

As a leader, it is important to own your own mistakes, accept responsibility, forgive yourself, and move forward. I spent my entire summer in school, that I paid for, with money from my window washing and grass cutting jobs. I never flunked another class and graduated on time. Excuses achieve nothing. If you want to achieve anything in life, you must work for it as no shortcuts exist, trust me, I tried.

Adversity rears its ugly head in the most damning places at the most damning times. When I was in the Air Force stationed at Kadena AB in Okinawa, Japan, I worked in the personnel office. My AF "uncles", George Jones, Tony Pinkney, and John Willie Sims groomed me to be an outstanding airman and furthered my education in manhood. Those men took me under their wings and showed me how to relate, how to adapt, the sequence of purchasing happy hour drinks at the enlisted club (very important to learn if you are to ever be invited to another), music, and the meaning of family during the holidays. I never spent one holiday alone in my dorm room because at least one of them would always have me at their homes for dinners.

I learned several things at Kadena and one was how to drive a stick shift. I did not know how to drive a stick-shift and I had no car. John Sims owned a 5-speed and taught me to drive it in one day. Kadena AB is a beautiful place full of tropical foliage, beautiful backdrops, and hills. John took me out to drive one day and told me to watch what he was doing. Now, picture this, in Japan, with a Japanese car, with the steering wheel on the right side and the stick assembly on the left. John drove me to the top of a hill, placed the car in neutral, pulled up the emergency brake and said, "Ok P, let's switch, you drive!".

WHAT?!!! We were at the top of the hill, all alone, at the stop sign. How in the heck was I supposed to drive this thing anywhere? Dare I remind you that I did not know how to drive a stick shift? As sweat poured down my back, I traded places, took the wheel, and began to try to drive the car. After rolling several feet backwards and jerking the car uncontrollably, I managed to drive down the street and back to the dorm. I learned through adversity to never give up. This lesson proved essential to my career progression in the Air Force.

When I worked in the personnel office, duly named the Consolidated Base Personnel Office (CBPO), I was tasked with filing papers in the records office and managing the in-processing briefing of new military members arriving at the base reporting to duty. When an opportunity came for me to be a Personnel Systems Manager (PSM), I quickly volunteered. I did not get selected and was told by my CBPO chief, Captain George Nixon that "As long as you are in my Air Force, you will never be a PSM". It turns out that Captain Nixon was wrong. Never let anyone tell you what you cannot achieve. If you are right, stick to your guns and see the process through, no matter how long or hard the journey.

My next assignment after Kadena was Fairchild AFB in Spokane, Washington in 1989. I worked in the CBPO in the manning control section. My manager, TSgt Ed Herring was very well versed in a word processing software called WordStar. He taught me WordStar inside and out and in doing so, he re-awakened my love of computers. TSgt Herring inspired me and supported my attempt to retry my transition to the PSM job. This time, I was successful, was scheduled to attend a retraining class at Keesler AFB in Biloxi, Mississippi, and started working half days in the PSM office learning on-the-job.

Between the time I was approved to attend PSM school and the class start date, the fiscal year changed and my school was canceled because the experience I gained on the job served as experience in lieu of the formal training I would have received in PSM school. My new CBPO chief, Major Cathy Hewitt called me into her office to give me the news. I was disappointed but she also said that I would be working full time in the PSM office and needed to immediately start my study for my "5" level. As God would have it, I learned PSM on the job from two of the AF PSM greats (of all time), MSgt Peter Belben at Fairchild and MSgt Tim Davis at my next duty station in England at RAF Lakenheath.

I left the Air Force in 1997 after 10 and a half years which included a 7-year stint as a PSM where I met several great people, learned my craft, was recognized as one of the best, earned a stripe, married my wife, and landed an excellent job as a technical analyst in Dallas, Texas when I was honorably discharged. To trace my story and tell of the many periods of adversity I have experienced in my life would take another entire book and I will write it one day, but this book is about leading from the inside out, which entails learning who you are. what your experiences taught you, and how those experiences have shaped your thinking. Part of learning yourself involves being transparent.

The stories I told speak to the need to be resilient through the many periods of adversity that you will experience in life. You should always remember those people you met along the way who helped shaped your life. I know many people, but hold only a few as friends with some being as close to me as brothers and are still in my life today. I only hold five men and three women in my inner circle today and they are the people that have been there for me in my times of need, comfort, truth, and humbling.

I met Kenneth Walker, a safety and emergency response guru in the Air Force at Fairchild AFB and held his daughter Lakendra in my hands when she was born. Ken provides sound counsel, strong support, and tells everything like it is. He never bites his tongue and I have yet to hear him complain about anything. He retired from the USAF as a SMSgt, transitioned to civilian service, and is now in Alaska affecting change. To date, he is my nearest brother running neck and neck with Greg Loyd.

I met Greg when I worked as a contractor at Mobil Oil and he was the catalyst that made me finish my college education. I was complaining that I had to help educated geologists who could not understand how to work on their computers and wondering why they were paid so much to know so little (in my mind). I told Greg that I was smart. He answered, "they have degrees, you don't, and if you are so smart, why haven't you finished your degree?".

I was LIVID, but enrolled in school that day and did not stop until I graduated with a Ph.D. with honors. It took me 16 long years, but I finished. I also consider Greg a brother and if you ever see me in Dallas, he is usually right beside me passing down knowledge to help me navigate through life. As an ex-Army captain, he too provides sound counsel, strong support, and tells me everything like it is. Notice a pattern here amongst my friends?

John Johnson; or young Johnson, as I affectionately call him is the little brother in the bunch and is the only civilian man in my inner circle. He very accomplished, smart, and is usually my good side. He can calm me down in my ignorant moments and speaks logic to make me think before acting, much like Ken and Greg. He can be found on the field coaching sports, on a ladder at his home, on his laptop, or at the barbeque grill. He too provides sound counsel, strong support, and tells me everything like it is.

My female friends Angela and Jennifer speak to my kinder, gentler side of thinking and have taught me over the years that it is not always brute strength that wins the day. Both are strong, independent women who provide sound counsel, strong support, and tell me everything like it is. Finally, is my friend Cynthia. A high school classmate, Cynthia was the cheerleader (an actual cheerleader) who talked to the nerd (me). She is still my close friend today and can be seen on Sundays in the choir at Calvary Revival Church in Norfolk, VA with the same signature smile she had in high school. She provides sound counsel, strong support, and tell.... well I am sure you get the point.

What was the purpose of exposing you to a bit of my life? What does that have to do with the title of this book? Leading from the inside out involves understanding how the culmination of events, choices, adversity, and people in your life put you where you are right now. One thing that I referenced in the beginning of this chapter is God's Plan and how acceptance of His Plan is both frightening and enlightening at the same time.

I am a Christian and I would be remiss and completely naive if I did not acknowledge God and what He has done for me in my short years here on earth. Yes, I am where I am because of the choices I made during my 48 years and God's gentle guidance. As I look back on everything, I can now more clearly see God's hand in my maturation, my safety, my thinking, my experiences, and my life. The Bible says in Matthew 10:33 "But whoever denies Me before men, I will also deny him before My Father who is in heaven". I will not deny.

As a leader, you are called upon to serve in many different capacities and you need to find a center to continue to be your best. Your center is your spiritual base or solemn refuge. It is the place that you return to reset your mind at times of chaos, conflict, confusion, and discomfort. During rough days, gradually clear the clutter from your mind and continually return to your center. Many people find their center in some sort of religious or spiritual base which gives them the inner peace. As a Christian, I am ever aware that my center is God.

I have learned that prayer is powerful and that it works. As the saying goes, most people are saved by the prayers of the righteous. The Bible states in James 5:16 "Therefore, confess your sins to one another, and pray for one another so that you may be healed. The effective prayer of a righteous man can accomplish much". I believe that I have been protected from disaster by the many prayers of my late grandmother, Norma McNair who I considered to be a prayer warrior.

Finding your center is different from clearing your mind in that when you find your center, you attach or surrender yourself to something bigger than you. You allow yourself to be consumed by the overall sense of transcending your mind to another level, another space, another dimension that only you can understand. To find your center is a personal endeavor at best and establishes a relationship with whatever you define as your spiritual center. Your center can never be taken from you, no matter what you go through personally.

Once you find your center; whatever it may be, create a routine to return to your center daily upon awakening and again before you retire for any extended periods of sleep. You must repeat this routine daily with an urgency of purpose and determination to succeed. Please understand that even when I found my center, I did not do everything right and I still run into adversity from time to time. The key to remember here is that adversity is no match for God or His plan he sets in place for you. It is our responsibility to take the initiative to seek and keep a constant connection with Him to live His Will.

I hope that this book helps someone. My goal was to help people understand that the real work in leadership is being able to understand and change yourself before you attempt to change others' lives. If you seek to understand who you are, your actions will attract those who grow to admire and follow you. Your work in understanding self and helping others does the same.

I believe that all people are leaders in some aspect of their lives, but that each person has a specific ministry to fulfill while walking the earth. The Bible says in Romans 12:6-8, "Since we have gifts that differ according to the grace given to us, each of us is to exercise them accordingly: if prophecy, according to the proportion of his faith; if service, in his serving; or he who teaches, in his teaching; or he who exhorts, in his exhortation; he who gives, with liberality; he who leads, with diligence; he who shows mercy, with cheerfulness".

Find your purpose, work to fulfill that purpose, and learn to lead, from the inside out. I am sure that if you stick to the principles that I laid out in this book, you will be well on your way to achieving your goals. I love you all.

WORKS CITED

Bass, Bernard M., and Ronald E. Riggio. *Transformational Leadership*. 2nd ed. New York, NY: Routledge, 2014. Print.

Paul, Richard W., and Linda Elder. *Critical Thinking: Tools for Taking Charge of Your Professional and Personal Life*. Upper Saddle River, NJ: Pearson Education, Inc, 2002. Print.

Rich, Preston B. *The impact of the relationship between ethical leader behavior, transformational leadership, and organizational performance moderated by organizational hierarchy* (2014) Print.

ABOUT THE AUTHOR

Dr. Preston Rich is a proud father, veteran, speaker, educator, transformational leadership consultant, management advisor, and entrepreneur in Frisco, TX. He served over 10 years in the United States Air Force which included two tours in support of Operation Desert Storm. He was a 2013 and 2015 Presidential Management Fellow (PMF) finalist. His diverse background has provided him with over 30 years of leadership experience in five separate industries. Dr. Rich currently imparts knowledge; as an adjunct professor, to management and organizational behavior students at Richland College in Dallas, TX. He has also taught management courses as a full-time faculty member at Collin College. His engaging, Socratic style has earned him the distinction as a "professor of choice" among the business student population on all campuses where he has taught. He recently developed the "Rich Thinking Series" designed to teach people how to use critical thinking to change and take control of their lives. He was the first scholar in the world to develop an instrument that quantitatively measured the relationship between ethical leader behavior and organizational performance. Dr. Rich is dedicated to positively impacting people by teaching them how to become transformational in all aspects of their personal and professional lives.

Made in the USA
Lexington, KY
19 August 2017